STORIES FROM SHAKESPEARE

CEFR level **A2**

Adapted by Read Stories – Learn English

Read Stories – Learn English

Stories from Shakespeare A2
Original texts by William Shakespeare
Adapted text © Karen Kovacs, 2023
Logo © Karen Kovacs, 2023

No part of this book may be reproduced, scanned or distributed in any printed or electronic form without permission. Please do not participate in or encourage piracy of copyrighted materials in violation of the author's rights. Thank you for respecting the hard work of the author.

CONTENTS

Meet the author   Page 4

People in the stories   Page 6

Macbeth   Page 9

Twelfth Night   Page 41

More stories   Page 76

Words from the stories   Page 78

Meet
the author

My name is Karen.

- I was born and brought up in England.
- I have a Master's degree in Linguistics.
- I have a teaching diploma and many years' teaching experience in the UK and abroad.
- I've written lots of books for learners of English.
- I speak Hungarian, French and Spanish so I understand what it's like to learn a foreign language!

Karen Kovacs

ReadStories-LearnEnglish.com

More stories at the same level

A SERIES OF MODERN CRIME THRILLERS

Book 1: **Hushabye**
ELT Graded Reader

Book 2: **Requiem**
ELT Graded Reader

Book 3: **Imago**
ELT Graded Reader

—The Kate Redman Mysteries—

Scan here to buy

New words

When you see a word in **bold**, go to the back of the book. There you will find a definition of the word.

People in the stories

Macbeth

Duncan – King of Scotland

Malcolm – Duncan's son

Macbeth – **Thane** of Glamis

Lady Macbeth – Macbeth's wife

The three **witches**

Banquo – a thane and Macbeth's friend

Fleance – Banquo's son

Macduff – a thane

Lennox – a thane

Twelfth Night

Viola (Cesario) – a **twin**

Sebastian – a twin

Lady Olivia

Sir Toby – Lady Olivia's uncle

Sir Andrew – Sir Toby's friend

Malvolio – Lady Olivia's **servant**

Maria – Lady Olivia's servant

Duke Orsino

Antonio – a sea **captain**

Macbeth

Chapter 1

One day, during a terrible **storm**, three old **witches** were talking.

"When shall we meet again?" one witch asked the others, shouting above the noise of the wind.

The second witch looked up, her hair wet from the rain. "Let's meet on the field after the **battle**," she answered.

"That will be before night time," said the third witch. She knew that because witches can see the **future**. Then she said, "We'll meet Macbeth there."

The witches said goodbye to each other. Then they flew away through the dark fog.

Duncan, the King of Scotland, was waiting at his castle for news of the battle between Scotland and Norway. When a young soldier came back from the battlefield,

Duncan asked him, "Who won? Tell me!"

"The battle was very long and very difficult," the soldier told his king. "But we're very lucky because we have a brilliant **soldier**, Macbeth. He killed lots of men and, because of him, we won!"

"That's brilliant!" shouted the King happily.

"And Banquo **fought** very well, too. But sadly," said the young man, "I also have bad news. One of our soldiers, the **Thane** of Cawdor, didn't fight for his country in the battle. He helped Norway instead."

Duncan was a good and kind king but, when he heard this, he became very angry. He shouted, "The Thane of Cawdor is Scottish but he fought with Norway? Then he's a **traitor** and he must die! My men will kill him."

"But who will be the new Thane of Cawdor?" a thane asked.

King Duncan thought for a moment. "Macbeth," he said, smiling. "He was the best soldier in the battle today. He's already Thane of Glamis and now he will be Thane of Cawdor too." The King was very pleased with his idea.

While the men were talking at the castle, the three witches met again, this time on the battlefield. There was another storm and it was very windy. They waited for Macbeth.

Macbeth and Banquo, both soldiers and good friends, were walking across the field **towards** the King's castle. It was getting dark and they were tired after the battle. **Suddenly**, they saw the witches. "Who are those strange women?" asked Banquo quietly. He was afraid. "They look so old and they're wearing really strange clothes. Are they real?"

"I don't know," said Macbeth. The witches were all looking at him with small, bright eyes. He was also a little afraid but he didn't want to show it. The men moved nearer and Macbeth asked them, "Who – or *what* – are you?"

They didn't answer him. "Say something!" Macbeth shouted, and then finally the women spoke.

"Macbeth, Thane of Glamis!" said the first witch, her arms in the air.

"Macbeth, Thane of Cawdor!" said the second

witch.

"Macbeth, the future king!" said the third witch.

Macbeth didn't understand. "I *am* Thane of Glamis, that's true. I became Thane of Glamis when my father died. But I'm not Thane of Cawdor so why do you say that? And how can I become king? That's not possible."

The witches said nothing. They just looked at him.

"Don't look so afraid," Banquo said, putting his hand on his friend's arm. "It's good news." Then to the witches, he said, "Do you have anything to say to *me*? What's *my* future?"

The witches all turned to look at Banquo, and one said, "You're less important than Macbeth … but you're also *more* important."

"What does that mean?" asked Banquo, **confused**.

"You won't be king," another witch explained, "but you will be the *father* of kings."

The witches started to **disappear**. "Wait!" shouted Macbeth. "We have more questions for you!" But the women were gone.

"Where did they go?" asked Banquo, looking

around him.

"They have disappeared into the air," answered his friend. Then he said to him, "Your children will be kings."

"*You* will be king," said Banquo.

"And Thane of Cawdor. They said that, too, didn't they?" asked Macbeth.

"Yes, they did."

While they talked, the men walked back to Duncan's castle.

When they entered the castle, King Duncan said to them, "Soldiers, I want to thank you both. You fought a fantastic battle today!" Then to Macbeth, he said, "You're my best soldier so I have decided that you're the new Thane of Cawdor."

"Thank you," said Macbeth, surprised, "but how is that possible? The Thane of Cawdor isn't dead."

"Yes, he is. He was a traitor and he fought with Norway, not us, so my men killed him," explained Duncan.

Macbeth walked to the other side of the room and

stood alone, thinking. "The witches were right – I am Thane of Cawdor now. So will I be King one day? Are they right about that too? This is all very strange."

Then Macbeth looked at his King and thought, "If I want to be king, I'll have to kill Duncan, but I don't want to do that." Then he had an idea. "Perhaps I can become king without killing him. I hope so."

Suddenly, Macbeth heard that Duncan was talking to him. "Macbeth, are you listening?" he said loudly to his favourite soldier, "I said, let's all go to your castle at Inverness tonight."

"Yes, good idea. You'll be very welcome," answered Macbeth.

He tried very hard to smile because he didn't want the King to guess his dark thoughts. But he wasn't happy. "Duncan is king now," he thought, "and Malcolm, his son, will be next. So how can I ever become king? I'll have to kill two men. Oh, I hate these horrible thoughts in my head!"

Macbeth arrived at his castle before everyone else and went to see his wife, **Lady** Macbeth. He told her all about the witches.

"And those three strange women were right," he said, "because I *am* Thane of Cawdor now."

"Thane of Glamis and Cawdor!" Lady Macbeth was very pleased and she put her arms around her husband. Then she stopped smiling and said, "You're quite **ambitious**, I know, but you're also too kind. Listen to me – you may have to do bad things but you *will* become king. Do you hear me? The witches told you that and they know the future."

Macbeth kissed his wife, then said, "My love, Duncan is coming to the castle tonight. He and the thanes are staying for one night."

His wife looked at him with a cold smile and said, "Duncan will never see tomorrow."

Macbeth looked back at her, surprised and upset. "He's a good king and he's my friend. I don't want to kill him."

"Yes, you do," said his wife, looking into his eyes, "but you're too afraid."

She was right. He wanted to be king but, for the first time in his life, he felt very afraid.

Duncan and the thanes arrived soon after this conversation. "Welcome!" said Lady Macbeth with a big smile.

"Your castle is lovely," said the King. "Your gardens are full of birds and the air here is clean and fresh. It's wonderful."

"Thank you, King Duncan," said Lady Macbeth. Then, to everyone, she said, "Dinner is ready so please follow me to the dining room."

The Macbeths and their guests all sat down around the long table and started eating but, after a few minutes, Macbeth hurried from the room.

Lady Macbeth went to find him. "What are you doing?" She spoke quietly but she was angry. "We have to be friendly to Duncan because he mustn't know that we want to kill him."

"How can I eat at a time like this? I'm feeling too worried. I don't want to kill him."

"Don't be a **coward**," Lady Macbeth said, holding both his arms in her hands. "Be a man! Remember that you are ambitious. We'll kill him while he's sleeping and everyone will think that his **servants** did it."

Macbeth looked down at the ground then back at his wife. "Yes, alright – I'll do it," he agreed. "Let's go back and finish dinner."

Chapter 2

It was midnight and there was another storm outside. The guests were all in bed, except Banquo and his son, Fleance. They couldn't sleep so they were walking through Macbeth's dark, quiet castle. Suddenly Banquo heard someone and he took out his knife. "Who's that?"

"It's your friend, Macbeth," said a voice.

"I can't sleep," Banquo said to him. "I had a dream about the three witches."

"Oh, did you? I haven't thought about them," said Macbeth, but, of course, this wasn't true. "It's late now but we can talk about them tomorrow, if you like."

Banquo agreed, and then he and Fleance finally went to bed.

Now Macbeth was alone, and dark thoughts filled his head again while he moved towards Duncan's bedroom. Suddenly, he looked up and saw something in the air in front of him.

He looked at it carefully and thought, "Is this a knife?" He tried to touch it but his hands went through it. "Is it only in my **mind**?" he thought, confused.

Then he saw something red on the knife. "Ah, now there's blood on it!" he said. "My mind is seeing all this because I'm going to kill someone tonight."

Macbeth was really upset but he went to the door of the King's room. Lady Macbeth was waiting for him there. "There are two servants in Duncan's room," she said quietly. "I gave them lots of wine and now they're sleeping."

Macbeth went into the bedroom and came quickly out again. The knives in his hands had blood on them. "I've done it." But suddenly he looked worried. "Who said that?"

"What are you talking about?" asked his wife. "There's nobody here."

"I heard a voice," said her husband. "It said, 'Macbeth has killed sleep. He will never sleep again!'"

"Stop it! What's the matter with you?" said Lady

Macbeth **angrily**. "Just go back into Duncan's bedroom and put the knives next to his servants. Then everybody will think that *they* killed the King."

"I can't!" he answered. "I'm too afraid. I can't look at Duncan's dead body."

"What a coward! He's dead – he can't hurt you," his wife said. "Give me the knives. I'll do it. Go and wash your hands. No one must see the blood on them."

Alone again, Macbeth looked down at his hands. "All the water in the sea won't wash this blood from my hands."

Then he heard another noise. "What's that **knocking** sound?" It kept getting louder and he listened in the dark. "What's happening to me?" he thought. "I'm afraid of every noise now."

Lady Macbeth came out of the King's bedroom and said to her husband, "My hands are red like yours but I am not a coward like you."

Then she heard the sound too. "It's the front door," she told him. "Someone's knocking because they want to come in. Come on, let's go to our bedroom quickly and wash our hands."

A servant opened the door and two thanes, Macduff and Lennox, entered the castle. Macbeth came back downstairs with clean hands.

"Can I see the King?" Macduff asked Macbeth. "He wanted me to come and see him early this morning."

"He's in that room," Macbeth told him, pointing, "but he's still sleeping."

"It doesn't matter. I have to see him," said Macduff and he walked into Duncan's bedroom.

While he was in there, Lennox asked Macbeth, "Is the King leaving today?"

"Yes, he is."

"It was such a strange night," Lennox said. "The wind was so loud. 'It's shouting about **death**!' I thought. A dark and dangerous time is coming – I know it sounds crazy but … I can feel it in the air.'"

"It was a strange night, it's true," Macbeth answered.

Soon afterwards, Macduff ran out of the bedroom, shouting, "Someone has killed the King!"

"What?" said Macbeth, trying to look surprised.

"Wake up, everyone!" Macduff shouted.

The other guests and all the servants hurried to hear the bad news. Then Lady Macbeth came out of her bedroom and asked, "What's happening?"

"Someone has killed the King!" repeated Macduff.

"In our house?" said Lady Macbeth, her hand over her mouth. "Oh no! That's terrible!"

"If Duncan is dead," said Macbeth in a loud voice, "then I don't want to live!"

Malcolm, the King's son, came downstairs and the others explained everything to him. Malcom's face went white. "Who did it?" he asked.

Lennox took him into Duncan's bedroom and showed him. "These men did it. Look, their knives have blood all over them."

Macbeth said to the others, "I killed Duncan's servants."

"Why did you do that?" asked Macduff, surprised.

"I really loved Duncan and I was angry with the men. They were traitors," Macbeth explained.

"That's a strange thing to do," said Macduff.

At that moment, Lady Macduff shouted, "Oh, help

me!" and fell to the ground. Two of the men picked her up and carried her out of the room.

A short time later, some of the men were talking about the King's death. It was daytime but it was dark outside because the weather was so terrible. "Look," an old man said, "there's going to be a storm. Duncan is dead and the sky is angry."

"Why did those men kill Duncan?" someone asked.

"I think Malcolm paid them to do it," said Macduff. "He has left Scotland. Why did he do that, when his father has just died?"

"If Duncan's son has left the country, then Macbeth will become king," another man said.

And he was right. Macbeth became king that day.

Chapter 3

After he became king, Macbeth, his wife and some of the other men went to his new castle on Dunsinane Hill.

Banquo sat in one of the rooms, thinking. "Now Macbeth is Thane of Glamis, Thane of Cawdor and King of Scotland. The witches were right. And I think that he did something terrible to become king. But the witches told *me*, 'You will be the father of kings.' Were they right about me, too?"

A moment later, Macbeth came into the room and said to Banquo, "We're having a big dinner tonight and I want you to be there."

"I'd like that, thank you," answered Banquo. "I'm going to ride my horse for a few hours this afternoon but I'll be back for dinner."

"Is Fleance going with you?" asked the new king.

"Yes, he is," said Banquo.

"Alright. See you both later."

After Banquo left the castle, Macbeth thought, "He's the only person I'm afraid of. His son will be king, the witches said. I have no children so I've killed Duncan for Banquo's son!"

Macbeth went outside and walked to the back of the castle. There, he spoke to two big, strong men. They worked for him. "I want you to kill Banquo and his son, Fleance."

The men agreed and Macbeth went back inside the castle, thinking, "I've done one bad thing and I can't stop now. I have to do more."

It was almost night-time, and Macbeth's men were in a wood. They were waiting for Banquo and his son to return. Soon, the men saw them.

When Banquo and his son got off their horses, Macbeth's men ran towards them. They killed Banquo in less than a minute. Before he died, he shouted, "Fleance, run!"

It was dark and Macbeth's men couldn't see clearly. Fleance was able to leave safely – he was very lucky.

Macbeth, Lady Macbeth and their guests sat down at the long table for dinner. "Welcome, all of you," said Lady Macbeth, smiling.

Suddenly, Macbeth saw one of his men by the door and he went to talk to him. "There's blood on your face," he told him quietly.

"It's Banquo's," the man answered.

"Is he dead then?" asked Macbeth.

"Yes, he is."

"Well done. And you killed Fleance too, I hope?" Macbeth asked.

"I'm sorry, but Fleance ran away," said the man.

"Oh no," said Macbeth, worried. "The young man isn't dangerous now but he will be in the future."

After the man left, Lady Macbeth walked towards her husband and said, "Come back and eat with your guests."

"Yes, I'm coming," he answered. He walked back to the table, picked up a glass and, still standing, said loudly, "Good health to you all!" Then he said, "Banquo isn't here. He's late. I hope he'll join us soon."

"Why don't you sit down, King Macbeth?" asked Lennox.

"How can I?" said Macbeth, looking confused. "The table is full."

"Here's an empty seat," said Lennox, pointing to Macbeth's chair.

But at that moment, Macbeth's face went white. He saw the **ghost** of Banquo, sitting in his chair. "Who did this?" he asked, very afraid.

"What do you mean?" asked Lennox.

Macbeth started speaking to the ghost. "Don't say that I did it! It's not true!"

The guests started talking to each other quietly. "The King isn't well. What is he talking about?"

"Please," said Lady Macbeth, trying not to look worried, "stay in your seats. My husband will be well again in a moment."

Then she went to Macbeth and said, quietly but angrily, "What's the matter with you? Have you **gone**

mad?"

"Banquo is in my chair … but he's dead."

"Stop it!" said his wife. "You know that there's nobody there! You're a man and a soldier so stop talking like a child!"

"Look over there and you'll see!" said Macbeth, pointing to his chair. But at that moment, the ghost disappeared. "Oh, he's gone."

"He was only in your mind," his wife told him. "And now all our guests are looking at you." Then to her guests, she said, "Please leave now, everyone."

"Good night," they all said. "We hope that Macbeth feels better soon."

Soon after their guests left the room, Macbeth and his wife went to bed but Macbeth couldn't sleep. He felt too **guilty**.

Outside, Lennox was talking to another thane. "People say that Fleance killed his father and then ran away. But I think Macbeth killed Banquo."

"Yes, I agree," said the thane. "And I think he killed Duncan, too."

"Where is Macduff?" asked Lennox. "Macbeth invited him to dinner but he didn't come."

"Macduff doesn't like the King," said the thane, "so he has joined Malcolm in England. They're both staying with the English King and they're all planning to fight Macbeth."

Chapter 4

The next night, the three witches were waiting inside a small, dark house, not far from the castle. "Macbeth is coming tonight," one of them said. "Let's prepare some magic while we wait."

There was a fire in the middle of the room. The strange old women started dancing around it and, every few seconds, they threw something into it. While they danced, they said, all together, "A snake's eye, a bird's foot, cook them in the fire. A dog's ear, a baby's finger, cook them in the fire."

Suddenly, they stopped and looked up. "Macbeth is coming," one of them said. "I feel it."

She was right. A moment later, Macbeth knocked on the door and came in. He looked at the fire and asked, "What are you doing?"

"We can't explain it to you," they said.

"What's going to happen to me next? I need to know. I can't sleep because I'm so worried about the future."

"Watch and we'll show you," they said, pointing to the fire.

Macbeth watched, very afraid, and a ghost came out of the fire. It looked like a soldier. "Macbeth, be careful!" the ghost said. "Macduff is a danger to you."

"I know that already," Macbeth answered.

A second ghost came out of the fire. This one looked like a baby with blood on its body. "Don't worry. Nobody born from a woman can kill you," it told him.

"Then I don't need to kill Macduff," said Macbeth, pleased. "But perhaps I *should* kill him. Then I won't be afraid anymore and I'll be able to sleep again."

A third ghost came out of the fire. It was a boy dressed like a king and it said, "Don't worry. You won't die until Birnam Wood walks to Dunsinane Hill."

Now Macbeth felt even happier. "That will never happen. A wood can't walk!" he said, laughing. "But tell me one more thing – will Banquo's sons ever be kings?"

"Show him!" the witches told the ghosts. "Show him!"

Eight ghost kings moved up from the fire. Another ghost followed them.

"You look like Banquo," Macbeth said to the last ghost. "Go away!"

Banquo's ghost looked coldly at Macbeth and pointed to the other eight ghosts. "This means that Banquo's children will be kings, and his children's children. Is that true?" Macbeth asked the witches. "Oh no, this is terrible! I don't want to look."

Suddenly, the witches and the ghosts disappeared and Macbeth was alone.

The King left the little house and soon afterwards, he saw someone in the dark. "Who's that?" he asked.

It was Lennox. He said, "I've come to tell you something important. Macduff has gone to England. He and Malcolm are preparing for a battle against you."

Macbeth was surprised. He thought for a minute,

then he said, angrily, "He's a traitor! His wife and children are still in Scotland, in his castle in Fife. My men will go there and kill them all!"

The King wanted it so, of course, it happened. Macbeth's men went to Fife and, there, they found his wife and children and killed them all.

Soon afterwards, a thane went to England and told Macduff about his family. "What? All my lovely little children are dead?" he asked, crying. "And my wife?"

"I'm sorry to bring you such sad news," the thane said, "but yes, it's true."

Malcolm was there too. His hand on Macduff's arm, he said "I'm sure that you hate Macbeth, and I do too." Then he shouted angrily, "So we must kill him! The English King has given us thousands of soldiers and they're ready to fight. Let's go back to Scotland."

Chapter 5

At Dunsinane Castle that night, Lady Macbeth was walking around her bedroom, carrying a lamp. Her eyes were open and sometimes she talked to herself ... but she was sleeping.

She walked to a bowl and starting washing her hands.

"There's still blood on my hands," she said to herself. "Will my hands never be clean? The old man had so much blood in him!"

She was Queen but it wasn't making her happy. She was often alone – Macbeth didn't talk to her anymore – and her mind was full of horrible thoughts.

"Don't look so afraid," she said, still sleeping. She was talking to her husband but he wasn't there. "Banquo is dead and he won't come back. Come to bed. We've done terrible things but we can't change that now."

Outside the castle, the English soldiers met near Birnam Wood. Malcolm and Macduff were with them, and Lennox joined them too. He hated Macbeth, like everyone else.

"Where's the King?" Malcolm asked.

"He's in his castle," a soldier told him, pointing up at Macbeth's home. "He's preparing for battle but people say that he has gone mad."

"Of course he's gone mad," said Lennox. "He was too ambitious and he's killed lots of people so now he feels guilty."

"Let's kill him!" shouted a soldier. "Then Scotland can have a good, kind king again. We'll be traitors but for a good reason."

Macbeth's men told him about the English soldiers but he wasn't afraid. "Until Birnam Wood walks to Dunsinane Hill, I won't die," Macbeth said. "And Malcolm and Macduff were both born from women, so how can they hurt me? The witches were right before and they're right now too, I'm sure."

Down in Birnam Wood, Malcolm told the soldiers, "Each of you, take a **branch** from a tree and hold it in front of you. Then Macbeth and his men won't be able to see us when we start moving towards the castle."

While this was happening, Macbeth, in his castle, heard some women crying. "What's the matter with them?" he asked a servant.

"They're crying because the Queen has killed herself," the servant answered.

Macbeth loved his wife but he didn't feel sad at this news. Nothing mattered to him anymore. "I'm not surprised that she's dead," he said. "Life is so short and it means nothing."

Macbeth went to stand by the window. When he looked out, he saw something terrible – Birnam Wood was walking towards Dunsinane Hill. He couldn't believe it. "How is that possible?" he asked, confused. "'Don't worry until Birnam Wood comes to Dunsinane,' the witches said. And now, the wood is coming to Dunsinane. But I mustn't be a coward."

Macbeth decided to go down and join his soldiers. The English soldiers threw down their branches and the battle began.

A young, English soldier ran towards Macbeth. "I'm not afraid of you," Macbeth shouted in his face and then he killed him. "Ha! You see?" Macbeth said, standing over his body. "You were born from a woman so you couldn't kill me!"

Macduff looked for Macbeth on the battlefield and, finally, he found him. "You killed my whole family and now *you're* going to die!" he shouted.

The two men fought each other. Macbeth wasn't worried because he remembered the witches' words. "Nobody born from a woman can kill me," he said, smiling.

"But I wasn't born," answered Macduff. "Doctors cut me from my mother's body."

Macbeth stopped fighting and looked at Macduff, surprised and worried. "Those witches played word games with me," he said, "and they were right about everything. But it doesn't matter because I don't want to live anymore."

The two men started fighting again.

Soon afterwards, the battle was over. "We've won!" shouted Malcolm to all his soldiers and thanes. Everyone was really pleased.

"Where's Macduff?" Malcolm asked.

"There he is," someone said. He was walking towards them, with something in his hand. "What is he carrying?" the man asked, but nobody was sure.

Slowly, Macduff got nearer and suddenly someone shouted, "He's carrying a head!"

Macduff walked towards the group and, holding the head high in the air, he said, "Malcolm, I've killed Macbeth. *You* are King of Scotland now."

Everyone shouted happily, "King Malcolm of Scotland!"

Malcolm thanked them and then said, "Scotland's dark and dangerous time has finally ended and now we can all be happy again."

Twelfth Night

Chapter 1

A group of people were travelling by ship. The journey was long but the weather was good most of the time. Then, one day, black clouds **appeared** and a terrible **storm** began. Strong winds and big **waves** hit the ship again and again, and the passengers were very afraid. "Somebody, help us!" they shouted, but nobody could hear them.

The storm did not stop, and after an hour, the ship broke into two pieces. A young woman and the ship's **captain** held onto a piece of the ship and the waves slowly took them to a beach.

The young woman, Viola, stood up and walked onto the beach, wet and tired. She shouted, "Where's my brother?" She looked around but she couldn't see him and she started crying. "Oh no! He's dead!"

The captain followed her onto the beach. "Maybe

your **twin** didn't die," he said kindly. "I think I saw him holding onto another part of the ship."

"Where are we?" Viola asked.

"This is Illyria," the captain answered. "I know because I was born in this country."

Viola sat down on the beach, her face worried. "What can I do here? I don't know anyone in this place."

The captain sat down next to her and started to tell her about the country. "A **duke** lives here. He's called Orsino and he's a good man. He isn't married," explained the captain, "and he loves a woman called **Lady** Olivia, but she doesn't love him. She stays at home alone and does not see or talk to any men – she won't for seven years."

"Really? Why not?" asked Viola, surprised.

"Because her brother died and she is very sad about it. She wants to remember him and forget all other men."

"I have no family and I need money," Viola said. "I would love to work for Olivia as her **servant** but she wants to be alone." She thought for a moment. "I know

– I'll get a job with Duke Orsino instead. But a single **lady** should not work for a single man so, first, I need to **disguise** myself as a man. Will you help me, captain?"

"Of course," he answered.

"And please don't tell anyone that I am a woman."

"I won't," he said. "Come with me. I can show you the Duke's house."

Lady Olivia's uncle, Sir Toby, was staying at her house. He was a clever but **mischievous** man and he never did any work. He loved laughing, drinking and singing. Sir Toby had a friend called Sir Andrew. He was very stupid but also very rich. Sir Toby asked him to stay at Olivia's house with him because he wanted Sir Andrew to pay for everything.

That evening, the two men were getting **drunk** together as usual and singing songs too loudly.

Olivia's servant, Maria, went to talk to the men. "You're making such a lot of noise! Lady Olivia doesn't like it."

"She's too **serious** since her brother's **death**," Sir

Toby answered. "But I won't ever stop having fun! Come on, join us, Maria!" He took Maria in his arms and danced around the room with her, laughing. Maria started laughing too.

After a few minutes, Sir Toby sat down and picked up a glass of wine. Maria became serious again and said to him, "Lady Olivia isn't happy that you brought Sir Andrew to her house."

Looking sad, Sir Andrew said, "It doesn't matter because I'm going home tomorrow anyway."

"What? Why?" asked Sir Toby.

"I came here to marry your niece but she doesn't want to see me. She'll never be my wife. The Duke wants to **marry** her and I suppose she'll say 'Yes'."

"No, she won't! She doesn't **care** about the Duke!" shouted Sir Toby.

"Oh, really?" said Sir Andrew, his face **suddenly** happier. "Then I'll stay another month!"

"Yes!" **cheered** Sir Toby, his hands in the air. "We'll have great fun!"

Soon after the captain took Viola to the Duke's house,

she became his servant. He believed that she was a man. She wore trousers, had a man's hat and a new name, Cesario. Before, she was beautiful as a woman, and now, she was good-looking as a man.

Cesario quickly became the Duke's favourite servant. They talked often and he told her about his love for Lady Olivia.

One day, while some of Orsino's men were playing beautiful love songs, the Duke explained, "Olivia won't see me because her brother died so she wants to be alone. Of course, that's a shame for me, but … it's also wonderful."

"Wonderful?" said Viola.

"Yes because it shows that she really, really loved her brother. She has a kind heart." He **sighed** happily and then said, "When I see her, the air is full of music."

The Duke didn't know it but Viola felt the same way about *him*. She was **falling in love** with him but it only made her sad – she couldn't tell him and he loved Olivia, not her.

A moment later, the Duke said, "Cesario, you must do something for me. Go to Olivia and tell her that I love her with all my heart."

"I can't," Viola answered. "Lady Olivia doesn't want to see anyone and her door is always closed. You know that."

"Don't leave until she opens the door," he said.

"Alright," she agreed. "I'll try." But she really didn't want to.

When Viola, dressed as Cesario, arrived at the house, the servant Maria went to tell Lady Olivia. "There is a young man at the door?" Olivia asked. "What does he want? Is he the Duke's servant?"

"I don't know," answered Maria, "but he won't leave."

"Malvolio, come here." Malvolio was another of Olivia's servants. He was serious and very **vain**, and nobody liked him.

He walked towards Olivia with his nose in the air. "Yes, Lady Olivia?"

"Go and talk to the man at the door," she told him. "Tell him that he can't come in."

Malvolio left the room and went to speak to Cesario

at the front door but, very soon, he came back.

"I told the young man that you were ill," he said, "but he didn't leave. Then I told him that you were sleeping, but he still didn't leave."

"Tell him to go away," she answered.

"I tried that but he's still standing there."

"Oh, alright!" said Olivia, throwing her hands in the air. "Bring him in."

A minute later, Viola entered the room, dressed as a man. "Hello, Lady Olivia," she said politely.

Olivia looked at him carefully. "He's young and his voice is still like a woman's," she thought, "... but he's very good-looking."

Maria and Malvolio left the room, and Olivia said to Viola, "Why are you here? My servants asked you to leave but you didn't. That's very **rude**."

"I'm sorry, Lady Olivia," said Viola, "but I have an important message."

"It's from the Duke, isn't it? I already know that he loves me," said Olivia, looking bored and sighing. "The other day, he sent another servant here to tell me."

"He loves you very much," answered Viola, "and now I understand why. With your lovely, long red hair and your large grey eyes, you are very beautiful."

Olivia looked into Cesario's eyes for several seconds without speaking. Then she looked away and said, "I don't care that the Duke loves me. He's a kind, intelligent man and he's good-looking, but I don't love him. I've told him that many times."

"Then he will write love songs for you," Viola told her, "come to your house in the middle of the night, and sing them under your window. When he does that, maybe you will fall in love with him."

Olivia wasn't interested in the Duke but she was interested in this young man. He spoke so beautifully about love. She moved closer to him, took his hand and quietly asked, "Who are you?"

Viola quickly took back her hand. "That doesn't matter," she answered.

"Go back to the Duke and tell him that I don't love him," Olivia said. Then, smiling at Viola and looking into her eyes, she said, "If you like, come back and tell me his answer. I would like to see you again."

Chapter 2

Viola left the house very sad. "The Duke will be so upset when I tell him that Lady Olivia doesn't love him," she thought sadly.

She turned and looked back at the house. She could see Olivia at her window, watching her and smiling. Suddenly, she thought, "I think Olivia loves *me* instead! Oh no! She doesn't know that I'm not a real man – she only sees my disguise. Orsino loves Olivia, Olivia loves me, and I love Orsino." She sighed and said, "This is crazy! What am I going to do?"

Things soon became crazier. Late that night, Sir Toby and Sir Andrew were having another party at Olivia's house. They were making a lot of noise and drinking too much, as always. Then they started singing love songs ... very badly.

Maria ran into the room. "Be quiet," she said. "Your

singing is terrible!" The two men didn't listen to her. They kept singing. "You sound like cats!" Maria said. "Oh and look – now Malvolio is coming. He's angry with you."

Malvolio appeared in his night clothes and, in an angry voice, shouted, "Stop it! How can you be so rude? It's late and I'm trying to sleep. And Lady Olivia told me that she can't sleep because of you. This is her house, not a pub!"

Sir Toby didn't care. He started singing again, a large glass of wine in his hand.

"Stop it!" repeated Malvolio.

"You don't enjoy having fun, Malvolio," answered Sir Toby, "but other people do! Go away! And Maria, bring us more wine!"

Maria started moving towards the men with a bottle of wine but Malvolio stood between her and Sir Toby. He put out his hand and said, "No. Don't give them any more wine, Maria." Maria put the wine back down on the table, then Malvolio left the room.

"Malvolio's so vain. He thinks that he's better than us but he's not," said Maria after Malvolio was gone.

Then she put her hand on Sir Toby's arm and said, "Sir Toby, let's be quiet now. Your niece needs to sleep."

Sir Toby smiled at her. "Alright," he agreed.

They all sat down together. A minute later, Maria said, "I have a brilliant idea!"

"What is it?" asked Sir Toby, excited to hear it.

"We're going to **trick** Malvolio!" she said mischievously. "I will write him a letter. He'll think it is from Lady Olivia because I'll write her name at the end."

Sir Toby laughed and said, "What will the letter say?"

"You'll see," she answered. Then she sat down and started writing.

The next morning, Maria, Sir Toby and Sir Andrew followed Malvolio out into the garden. Maria had the letter in her hand. She put it down on the garden path and then they all **hid** behind a tree. Soon, Malvolio walked that way. He couldn't see the others.

While he walked, Malvolio was talking to himself. "I think Lady Olivia loves me. She always speaks more kindly to me than to the other servants."

The others heard this and laughed quietly from behind the tree. "He's so vain," said Sir Toby.

Malvolio kept talking, not knowing that they were listening. "If I marry her, I'll be rich and important."

"He's only a servant. He can't marry my niece!" said Sir Toby. "I'm going to hit him!"

"No. Be quiet," Maria told him. "He'll find the letter in a minute – just wait and watch."

"After our **wedding**, I'll be the man of the house," Malvolio said, "and I will say to Olivia's terrible drunk uncle, 'Toby, you must stop drinking. And your stupid friend must leave my house.'"

"Is he talking about me?" asked Sir Andrew, stupidly.

"Yes, of course," answered Sir Toby. "He's so rude."

Then suddenly Malvolio saw the letter. "What's this?" he said to himself. He picked it up and started reading it in a loud voice.

Dear M

I love you and I want you to know, but we mustn't tell anyone else. I am your lady but soon, I hope, you will be my man.

*Do you love me too? If you do, show me! Be rude to the other servants and to my uncle, smile all the time ... and please, wear your yellow **stockings**!*
Your Lady O

After reading the letter, Malvolio thought about the meaning of it and then said, "Yes, I understand. I am 'M' and Lady Olivia is 'Lady O', and she's telling me to show my love for her by wearing my beautiful yellow stockings. Then she will know that I want to marry her!" He smiled and kissed the letter. Then he said, vainly, "I knew she loved me."

The others laughed but Malvolio didn't hear them. He walked slowly back into the house and the others came out from behind the tree.

"Well done, Maria! That was a fantastic letter," Sir Toby told her. "Malvolio really believes that Olivia wrote it."

"Yes! We tricked him!" said Sir Andrew.

"He's going to look so stupid in those ugly, bright stockings," said Sir Toby, "and Olivia hates the colour yellow!"

"The letter told him to smile a lot," Maria said, "but Lady Olivia is sad at the moment so she'll be angry with him."

They all laughed and went back into the house.

Chapter 3

Soon afterwards, Viola, dressed as Cesario, went back to Lady Olivia's house. Olivia came out to see her and Viola told her, "I have another message from Duke Orsino."

"I don't want to hear any more messages from him!" Olivia said, **angrily**. Then she took Viola's hand in hers and looking into her eyes, said, "I can't hide my love anymore – I love you, Cesario!"

Viola moved back, surprised, and said, "I will never marry a woman." Then she quickly said goodbye and left.

Two men were walking on the beach and talking. One was a captain called Antonio, a strong man with a kind face. The other was a young man called Sebastian.

"Thank you for finding me, Antonio, and bringing

me in your boat to Illyria," said the younger man. "I nearly died in those waves." He looked at the sea, trying hard not to cry.

He was sad and the captain knew the reason. "I'm sorry I couldn't find your sister as well," he said.

"My father died a few years ago," explained Sebastian. "I was so upset but at least I still had my twin sister. We were very close. Of course, she was a woman and I am a man but people always said that we looked like each other."

They kept walking along the beach. A few minutes later, Antonio asked his new friend, "Where are you going to go? What are you going to do?"

"You told me about Duke Orsino," answered Sebastian. "Maybe he can help me. I'll go to his house."

"I can't come with you," said Antonio.

Sebastian looked at him, surprised. "Why not?"

"Orsino and his men all hate me," the captain said, "because we had a **battle** at sea many years ago. If I go to his house, they might kill me."

"Oh!" said Sebastian. "That's terrible."

"Do you have any money?" Antonio asked.

"No, I don't," answered his friend. "My money was all lost in the storm."

"Here," said Antonio and he gave him his wallet.

"You're a good friend. Thank you again," said Sebastian, his hand on Antonio's arm. "We must say goodbye now."

"It's dangerous for me to be near Orsino," said the captain, "but you're my friend – if you need me, I'll always help you."

Sebastian thanked him for his kind words and then left.

Olivia was in a chair by the window, thinking about Cesario and sighing sadly. "I want to see him again but how can I?" she thought. "Maybe Malvolio will have a good idea. He's very serious and will think carefully about the problem." She shouted Malvolio's name and he hurried into the room. He was wearing bright yellow stockings, a big smile on his face.

Maria was walking past the room and she saw Malvolio in his stockings. "He's trying to show Olivia that he read the letter but she doesn't know anything about it!" she thought. Quickly, she went to get Sir Toby and Sir Andrew and they all hid in a corner of the room and watched.

When Lady Olivia saw Malvolio, she stood up and put her hands over the mouth. "What's the matter with you? You never smile! And what are you wearing? Are you crazy?"

"You told me to smile, my dear Lady Olivia," he answered. "And you told me to wear these wonderful stockings." He pointed to his legs. "You see?" Then he moved towards her and tried to kiss her hand.

"Go away!" she shouted. "You're being very rude!"

She started to leave the room and then saw Maria and the others. "Maria, Uncle Toby, listen," she said. "Malvolio has **gone mad**. Go and look after him, please." They agreed and Olivia went upstairs to her bedroom.

Malvolio heard the conversation and thought, "Ah, she's worried about me. It's easy to see that she loves me."

Sir Toby and the others walked towards Malvolio.

He remembered the letter (*"Be rude to the other servants and to my uncle"*) so he said, "What do you want? Don't talk to me – you're all stupid, lazy and drunk."

Sir Toby looked at Maria and said, smiling mischievously, "Let's put Malvolio in a dark room and close the door."

"Good idea," agreed Maria. "The house will be more fun without him."

After they put Malvolio in the room, Sir Toby sat down with his friend. Sir Andrew said, sadly, "I want to leave."

"Why?" asked Sir Toby, worried because he needed Sir Andrew's money.

"Lady Olivia loves Cesario – I've seen them together."

Sir Toby thought for a moment, then suddenly he had an idea. "Don't leave," he said. "Olivia will love you, you'll see."

"Will she? How? What should I do?" asked Sir Andrew, his eyes brighter now.

"Show her that you are **brave**!" Sir Toby told him. "Tell Cesario that you want to have a **duel** with him."

"A duel?" asked Sir Andrew, his face going white. "But, Sir Toby, I'm *not* brave. I've never fought anyone before and I'm afraid of having a duel. I might die!"

"You must do it," Sir Toby told him. "It will show Olivia that you love her." At that moment, he saw Viola walking towards the house. "Look, there's Cesario," he said, pointing out the window. "He's bringing another message for Olivia, I suppose. Let's go and talk to him."

Chapter 4

Sir Andrew didn't want to go with Sir Toby but the older man pulled him outside.

The two men appeared in front of Viola. "You're Cesario, is that right?" asked Sir Toby, looking mischievous.

"Yes, sir," Viola answered, suddenly worried.

"My friend Sir Andrew wants to fight you in a duel," he said, his hand on his friend's arm.

"What? Why? I don't want to fight anyone," Viola said. "I haven't done anything wrong."

"Of course you have," Sir Toby said but he didn't tell Viola the reason for the duel.

Sir Toby pushed his friend and Viola closer to each other. In Viola's ear, he said, "You will have to fight well because Sir Andrew has killed several men. He's a brilliant fighter." Then, in Sir Andrew's ear, he said,

"Be brave. He's young so he will be very quick."

Viola and Sir Andrew stood opposite each other. They were very afraid and they were both trying not to cry but they took out their **swords**.

Sir Toby stood in front of them and said loudly, "When I say 'Go!' you may start fighting."

Sir Andrew didn't want to fight. He wanted to run back inside the house. And Viola wanted to tell them that she was in disguise and that she was not a real man. But they didn't want to be **cowards** so they held their swords up.

Antonio was on the road, passing by the house. He was looking for Sebastian so, when he saw the group of men, he walked towards them. "Is that you, my friend?" he said to Viola. "Put down your sword! I'm stronger than you. I will fight this man instead."

"Who are you?" asked Sir Toby, confused.

Before Antonio could answer him, two policemen shouted, "There he is!" They ran towards Antonio and caught him. "We know it's you, Antonio. We remember you from the battle at sea. Duke Orsino told us to catch you if we saw you one day."

Very worried now, Antonio looked at Viola. "If I pay these policemen, maybe they won't take me to **prison**," he said. "Please give me some of that money."

"What money?" said Viola.

"I've been really kind to you," answered Antonio, "but now you won't help me?"

"I don't know you," said Viola. "But you tried to help me today, it's true, so here," and she gave him half of her money.

The policemen looked at the money and said, "That's not enough. Come with us – we're taking you to prison." They took Antonio by the arms and started walking away with him between them.

"I don't understand you, Sebastian," Antonio shouted back at Viola. "I thought you were my friend but I was wrong."

Viola watched the men leaving and thought happily, "That man thought I was Sebastian because, in these clothes, I look like him. That means he knows my brother! So Sebastian isn't dead!"

Sebastian was in the town, looking for something to

eat. He was having a terrible time because people kept calling him the wrong name. A shop assistant shouted to him, "Hello, Cesario! How are you?"

Sebastian looked at him but didn't answer. "Why does he think my name is Cesario?" he thought. "I don't understand it. Illyria is a very strange place."

Sir Andrew and Sir Toby saw him and went to talk to him. "Cesario, what are you doing here?" asked Sir Toby.

"I'm not Cesario! What are you talking about?" answered Sebastian, confused.

"If you're not Cesario," Sir Toby said, laughing and pointing to his own face, "then this is not my nose."

"I don't know you!" Sebastian shouted. "Go away!"

Sir Andrew moved suddenly towards Sebastian and said, "Cesario, I have something for you!" Sebastian looked at him. Sir Andrew shouted, "Here it is!" and hit Sebastian in the face.

Sebastian hit Sir Andrew back and said, "Is everyone crazy in this town?"

The two men kept hitting each other and then Sir Toby joined in the fight. "I'll hold Cesario's arms," he said to his friend. "Then you can hit him more easily. Go on!"

"Stop it!" shouted Sebastian. He pulled his arms away from Sir Toby and took out his sword. "Let's have a duel," he said.

Sir Toby took out his sword too and the two men stood opposite each other, ready for a fight.

At that moment, somebody shouted, "No! Uncle Toby, put down your sword!" It was Lady Olivia and she ran towards the three men. "What are you doing?" she asked her uncle angrily. "Go home, both of you!"

Sir Toby and Sir Andrew walked away. Then, to Sebastian, Olivia said, "Are you alright, Cesario?" She smiled kindly at him and looked into his eyes. "Come back to the house with me and I will look after you."

Sebastian smiled back at her, feeling really happy. "I don't know this woman but she is really beautiful," he thought. He put his arm through hers and said, "Alright, let's go."

When they arrived back at the house, Olivia smiled at him and said, "Let's get married! There's a church close to the house."

For a moment, Sebastian was too surprised to answer. He was thinking, "Have I gone mad? Or is Lady Olivia mad? She wants to marry me but I don't know her! Am I dreaming? Is this all a big mistake? My friend Antonio isn't here so I can't ask for his advice. What should I do?"

Lady Olivia didn't want to wait. "Come on," she said. "Let's go!"

Sebastian looked at Olivia's beautiful face. "I'm so lucky!" he thought. "I don't understand all this but Olivia is wonderful and I never want to leave her."

Holding hands, they walked to the church together.

Chapter 5

Two hours later, Duke Orsino arrived at Lady Olivia's house. He was there to see her and Viola was with him. While they were waiting outside, Viola saw Antonio with the two policemen, walking along the road.

"That man helped me," she said, pointing at him.

The Duke looked at the captain, his face angry. "I know that man! He fought against me and my men in a battle at sea." He walked towards Antonio and shouted, "What are you doing here?"

"There was a storm at sea and that young man," Antonio answered, pointing at Viola, "was dying in the waves. I brought him in my boat to Illyria. Then I helped him a second time – another man wanted to fight a duel with him but I said, 'I will fight that man instead.' And now, he says he doesn't know me and he won't give my money back!"

"I don't understand," said Viola, looking up at Duke Orsino. "I don't know him."

Orsino turned to Antonio. "You're crazy," he told him. "This man is my servant and he has worked for me for three months. He has never met you before." To the policemen, he said, "Take him away."

Olivia saw them all from her window so she came out to join them. While she was walking towards them, Duke Orsino said quietly to Viola, "Here is the most beautiful woman in the world." He turned to Olivia and started to speak to her. "My dear lady, …"

But Olivia stopped him and said, "No, Orsino! I don't want to hear it."

"You're always so rude to me," said the Duke with sad eyes.

Olivia didn't answer him. Instead, she looked at Viola and said, upset, "I was looking for you everywhere! Why did you leave the house?" She hurried towards the twin and tried to put her arms around her.

"I wasn't in the house," Viola told her, pushing Olivia away. "What are you talking about?"

"You're my husband!" Olivia said. "We just got married."

"Husband?" Orsino asked, confused.

"Yes," answered Olivia.

"I'm not your husband!" said Viola.

The Duke didn't believe Viola and he was very upset. "Why did you marry Lady Olivia? You know I love her. You're the worst servant and the worst friend. I never want to see you again!"

Viola looked at the Duke and then at Olivia, really confused. "No, please, it's not ..." she started to say.

At that moment, Sir Andrew appeared with Sir Toby. "Help him, help him!" Sir Andrew shouted, pointing at Sir Toby and showing everyone the blood on the older man's head. "Cesario hit him!" he said, looking angrily at Viola. "And he hit me too!"

"Cesario?" Olivia and Orsino both said, not able to believe it.

"I didn't ..." Viola started to say.

She couldn't finish because Sir Andrew said, "We thought Cesario was a coward but we see now that he isn't."

"What are you talking about?" Viola said to him. "You tried to fight a duel with me but I didn't hurt you."

"Maria!" shouted Lady Olivia and her servant joined them. "Take my uncle and Sir Andrew to their bedrooms and give them some medicine. They are hurt."

While Sir Toby and Sir Andrew were walking back into the house, Sebastian was walking out. He went towards his wife. "I'm sorry, my dear," he said sadly. "I hurt your uncle and his friend but they started the fight, not me." He saw that Lady Olivia looked really confused and he said, "You're looking at me very strangely so I suppose that you're angry with me. I'm really sorry." He kissed her hands.

Orsino was watching Sebastian with wide eyes. "One face, one voice, the same clothes ... but two people."

Then Sebastian saw Antonio. He smiled and said, "My friend! There you are!"

"Sebastian," answered the captain, "is it really you?"

"Of course it's me!" Sebastian said, laughing.

"But there are two of you!" Antonio said, looking from one twin to the other.

Lady Olivia sighed happily and said to herself, "Ah, there are two of them. How wonderful!"

Sebastian turned and saw Viola for the first time. His mouth opened in surprise. Then he said to her, "Is that me standing there? I never had a brother. I had a sister but the strong waves killed her. Who are you? Are we family?"

"I come from Messaline," answered Viola. "My father was called Sebastian, and my brother had the same name but he died at sea."

"You're not a woman so you're not my sister," said Sebastian sadly.

But Viola took off her man's hat and, for the first time since she arrived in Illyria, everyone saw her long hair. She held her hands out to her brother. He ran to her and put his arms around her, crying. Then he turned to Olivia and said, "You were tricked, my dear, but it doesn't matter. We're married now and I'm so happy to be your husband." Olivia took his hand and smiled at him.

Orsino looked at Viola and said, "I love spending time with you and I always wanted a woman like you. Do you love me?"

"Yes!" Viola answered, looking into his eyes.

"Then let's get married," Orsino said, smiling.

"I would love that!" Viola said and she kissed him. Then she pulled back and said, "But I will need my women's clothes."

"Malvolio can find them for you," Olivia said and she looked around for him. "Where is he? I haven't seen him for a long time."

Maria came back outside and said, "Malvolio's gone mad, Lady Olivia, so we put him in a dark room alone."

Olivia was angry when she heard this. "That's not kind. Bring him here now."

"Yes, Lady Olivia," said Maria.

Maria brought Malvolio into the front garden, and Sir Toby and Sir Andrew came with her too. When Malvolio came outside, his eyes hurting from the bright light of the sun, he walked towards Lady Olivia and said angrily, "Why did you send me this?" He showed her the letter.

Olivia was confused. She took the letter and read it. "I didn't write this. This is Maria's writing!"

Everyone looked at the mischievous servant but Sir Toby hurried to her and said, "Don't be angry with Maria. It was my idea to put Malvolio in the dark room."

Olivia looked at Malvolio. "Poor you," she said. "They really tricked you."

"I hate all of you!" Malvolio shouted at Sir Toby, Sir Andrew and Maria, his face red. He ran back into the house.

Sir Toby watched him, then turned to Maria and said, "It's so fun being with you. I've fallen in love with you. Will you marry me?"

"Yes, alright," Maria answered, laughing. "Why not?"

Duke Orsino walked towards Antonio and said, "Let's be friends. I don't want to fight you anymore." Antonio agreed.

Then the Duke took Viola's hand and, together,

they moved to the front of the group. Orsino smiled kindly at everyone and said, "There will be two weddings today!"

They all cheered happily and then walked back into the house.

More books

A1 / Elementary

A2 / Pre-intermediate

B1 / Intermediate

B2 / Upper intermediate

Scan here to buy

VISIT MY WEBSITE

You will find:
- **information** about my **other books**
- a **free story**
- **free exercises** for this book
  (vocabulary exercises, comprehension exercises and notes about British culture)

ReadStories-LearnEnglish.com

Words from the stories

ambitious (adj)
really wanting to be rich and powerful

angrily (adv)
in an angry way

appear (v)
start to be present, start to be seen

battle (n)
a fight between two armies

branch (n)
a part of a tree that grows from the main trunk and has leaves on it

brave (adj)
doing things that are dangerous or scary without feeling afraid

captain (n)
the person in charge of a boat or ship

care (v)
feel that something is important and feel worried about it

cheer (v)
shout loudly to show happiness or support

confused (adj)
not understanding something

coward (n)
not brave, not doing dangerous or scary things

death (n)
the end of life

disappear (v)
become impossible to see

disguise (v)
change your appearance to hide who you are (**disguise**, n)

drunk (adj)
unable to speak or behave in a normal way because you have had too much alcohol

duel (n)
a formal fight in the past using swords between two people who disagree about something

duke (n)
a man very high in a country's social hierarchy

fall in love (phr)
develop a strong romantic attachment

fight (v)
be in a war or battle against an enemy (**fight**, n)

future (n)
the time that will come after the present

ghost (n)
the spirit of a dead person that someone believes they can see

go mad (phr)
start to be mentally ill/crazy

guilty (adj)
feel ashamed because you did something bad

hide (v)
not show

knock (v)
hit a door because you want someone to open it

lady (n)
a woman from a high social class (**Lady**, n = a formal title for a woman from the nobility)

marry (v)
become the husband/wife of someone

mind (n)
the part of your body that helps you think and feel

mischievous (adj)
enjoying having fun, playing tricks on people and annoying/embarrassing them

prison (n)
a building where you keep prisoners

rude (adj)
not polite

serious (adj)
not smiling, laughing or joking much

servant (n)
a person who works in someone's house, cooking and/or cleaning

sigh (v)
breathe out/exhale loudly, to show you are sad, angry etc

soldier (n)
someone in an army who fights

stockings (n)
thin clothing for the legs, worn under other clothes

storm (n)
bad weather with thunder and lightning

stupid (adj)
not intelligent, or ridiculous

suddenly (adv)
quickly and unexpectedly

sword (n)
a weapon with a long metal part

thane (n)
a man who fought for the king and had a good position in society

towards (adv)
in the direction of

traitor (n)
somebody who does something that will harm their country/king/queen etc

trick (v)
make somebody believe something that is not true

twin (n)
one of two children born at the same time to the same mother

vain (adj)
too proud of your own appearance or abilities

wave (n)
a line of raised water in the sea that moves

wedding (n)
a marriage ceremony, with a meal and dancing afterwards

witch (n)
a woman with magic powers

www.ingramcontent.com/pod-product-compliance
Lightning Source LLC
Chambersburg PA
CBHW011959090526
44591CB00018B/2716